TALKING WITH HEDGEHOGS

THOUGHTS FOR THE DAY

Eddie Askew

By the same author:
A Silence and a Shouting
Disguises of Love
Many Voices One Voice
No Strange Land
Facing the Storm
Breaking the Rules
Cross Purposes
Slower than Butterflies (book and spoken word cassette)
Music on the Wind
Edge of Daylight (Memoirs)

Published by
The Leprosy Mission International
80 Windmill Road, Brentford
Middlesex TW8 0QH, United Kingdom

First published 2001
© A.D. (Eddie) Askew, OBE
© Paintings and drawings by the author

Scripture quotations taken from the
HOLY BIBLE, NEW INTERNATIONAL VERSION
© 1973, 1978, 1984 International Bible Society.

Editorial and Design by Craft Plus Publishing Ltd.
53 Crown Street, Brentwood, Essex CM14 4BD

Printed and bound in England by Stanley L. Hunt (Printers) Ltd., Rushden
A catalogue record for this book is available from the British Library.
ISBN 0-902731-45-9

Cover picture: Farm Cottage, Norway, *Watercolour*

Summer Sky, *Pastel*

To Peter and Howard
who make the family complete

Silver Birches, *Pastel*

Envy is not usually a word that crosses my lips but occasionally I have to confess that one of the seven deadly sins does creep into my consciousness. It's often when I'm in the studios of BBC Radio Nottingham capturing on our digital technology the pearls of well-grounded wisdom that spill from Eddie's lips as he takes me through the 'Thoughts' he so beautifully crafts for our Breakfast Show. Why envy, from someone who can trace his lineage in broadcasting some considerable way back into the 20th century? Easy – Eddie has that God-given skill of being able to encapsulate in just a few sentences an idea that speaks to all who hear. In the car, in the bathroom, at breakfast or even in the bedroom. No matter how great the distraction his words cut through with a precision that leaves me breathless with admiration.

This collection is a superb illustration of what I have taken far too many words to explain. And another thing, he can even illustrate his books as well. There's just no hope for me, a ham-fisted organist, is there?

Andrew David - Senior Producer, Religious Programmes, BBC Radio Nottingham.

Eddie Askew with Andrew David recording 'Thought for the Day' at the BBC Radio Nottingham studio.

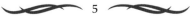

Why *Talking With Hedgehogs*? Well, why not? In broadcasting 'Thought for the Day' it's crucial to catch the listeners' attention immediately and hold it for one minute forty-five seconds. Give an uninteresting opening and you're lost. You just become background noise in competition with the morning traffic or the other demands of the day. Humour helps.

'Thought for the Day' also has to be earthed and must make a quick point that's relevant and helpful to people of all faiths and none. We all need a word to hang on to as another day begins, a thought that may help us through the hours ahead.

That's the challenge – but where does the inspiration come from? It can be words on a poster, glimpsed briefly as I drive by, or a phrase heard and remembered from a television programme. Mostly though, life itself provides the ideas. An experience travelling, a joke overheard, a conversation thought over at day's end, are all material to be identified and shaped for use. Imagination can take something ordinary and see a wider meaning in it.

Someone – I can't remember who – said, "If we are created in the image of the creator-God we are created creative." As a writer and a painter – I rarely call myself an artist, that's a judgement other people have to make when they see my work – it's a great thrill to share in that creativity. To think that through writing and painting, we share a tiny part of the great creative purposes of the God who reveals himself to us through Jesus Christ, and through the lives of those who try to follow him. I can only pray that these pages may help travellers on the way and encourage them to look for a deeper significance in what happens each day in their own lives.

Eddie Askew

"Come to me, all you who are weary and burdened, and I will give you rest. Take my yoke upon you and learn from me, for I am gentle and humble in heart, and you will find rest for your souls. For my yoke is easy and my burden is light."

Walking around the garden the other morning between rain showers I saw something move in the long grass. Rather too much grass about, at the moment. It was a hedgehog, looking a bit miserable in the damp. I watched him for a bit until I realised he was watching me.

"Good morning, hedgehog," I said. "Funny sort of life you lead. Just rooting around in the hedge all day, looking for food. Don't you get bored? Not much of a diet either, is it? Just worms, slugs and insects. I don't think I'd like to be a hedgehog."

The hedgehog thought for a minute. Then he said, "I know what you mean, but look at it from my point of view. When autumn comes, I'll find a nice quiet hole somewhere, snuggle up warm and go to sleep right through the winter. You'll be out there working, shovelling snow and fending off double-glazing salesmen."

It is true. Nature has its seasons. Times of intense activity when every waking hour is busy. Finding food, growing, bringing up young. Then comes a time of rest, when everything winds down, seems to relax.

The trouble is that we humans have lost this natural rhythm. We rush around the whole time because that's what life seems to demand of us. And then we wonder why we crack up. We're human, because that's the way God made us, and he knows that we can only do so much before we need a break. Relax.

Lord, slow me down.

> Very early in the morning, while it was still dark,
> Jesus got up, left the house and went off to a solitary place,
> where he prayed.

A thought came to me the other day. Just as well really as I'm supposed to provide them occasionally for this radio programme. There's no mention in the Gospels of Jesus ever running. I'm sure he did as a child, like other kids. My grandchildren run everywhere. And they only have two gears – fast and overdrive.

But a reference to Jesus running when he was grown up? No trace. Jesus and his disciples walked everywhere. No suggestion of any other form of transport. No carts or chariots. Now, it can be a bit dangerous drawing ideas from what isn't written or said – although we do it with politicians all the time – but it suggests to me that Jesus and his friends had time to spare.

Some of the journeys they made from Galilee to Jerusalem only take a few hours by tourist bus today, but for them it meant three or four days walk. It gave them time to think, to talk to each other, to look up at the sky and around at the hills and fields. And it gave them time for people.

We've lost a lot of that in the mad rush we call life. We move so fast that we have to keep our eyes on the road, with no time for the landscape or the people in it. A poet from my youth, W.H. Davies, wrote in his poem *Leisure*:
>   What is this life if full of care, we have no time to stand and stare.
>   No time to stand beneath the boughs and stare as long as sheep or cows.

If we stand and stare these days we're likely to be told to "move on, you're blocking the pavement". But we do need time to relax, time to think and pray, time for people. Take a moment today to stand, to look around, to talk to a friend.

> Lord, help me today to find a little space and time for people,
> and for you.

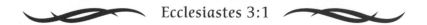

Ecclesiastes 3:1

*There is a time for everything, and a season for
every activity under heaven.*

A man who had worked hard all his life was asked what he would do in retirement. "For the first month," he said, "I'll sit on the porch in my rocking chair." "And then what?" "Then I'll start rocking – slowly," he answered.

Why do we find it so hard to slow down? Most of us aren't human beings any more, we're human *doings*. We rush around madly from one thing to the next. Achievement is all that counts. We show each other full diaries, shake our heads and say we wish we had more spare time, but secretly we enjoy the thought that the world can't get along without us. That if we didn't do things, the earth would grind to a halt. That we are indispensable.

But this constant activity leaves us little time to look at who we are or where we're going. No time to think. A wise writer in the Bible said that there's a time for everything under the sun – and I reckon that includes a time to release ourselves, let go and recharge our batteries.

"Be still and know that I am God," the Psalmist advises. It means 'relax and know ...'. The problem with our frenetic activity is that it crowds God out. We think our busyness is on his behalf, but really it pushes him to the edge of our lives. Take time out today, relax and give God a chance to make himself felt.

*Lord, when life is fast and I am getting breathless,
help me to feel your presence
in the pressures.*

Overleaf:
Loch Long, *Pastel*

A.D.ASKEW

For the revelation awaits an appointed time ... though it linger
wait for it; it will certainly come and will not delay.

It was early spring. I was working in the garden, moving a pile of old bricks rescued from when we repaved the driveway. Hidden in a space between two of the bricks I found a dusty, grey cocoon. Last autumn a caterpillar had fattened itself up by eating into my shrubbery. It had found somewhere to hide, spun its protection against the winter – and hibernated.

As I looked at it, it seemed dead, totally inert with nothing happening. But in the secrecy of the cocoon, changes were taking place. Gradually, quietly, mysteriously, the caterpillar inside was being transformed. In a few days, the restrictive cocoon would split and a new creature would emerge. A butterfly or moth – I can't identify cocoons – would unfold its wings and fly into a freedom it had never known. Its waiting time over.

I wonder sometimes about what really happened on the first Easter Saturday. I know about the drama of Good Friday and the joy of Easter Sunday, but what about the day in between? The day when nothing seemed to be happening. The day the disciples were mourning for what had been and didn't yet know what would be.

Even then, things were happening unseen and unknown in the cocoon of God's purposes. Events that would shake the world and change it more powerfully than anything else, events that would give us the freedom to live as nothing else could. All that was needed was time.

Waiting can be hard, but little happens without it.

Lord, let me glimpse your purpose in the mystery of life.
And when the mist descends, help me to wait in patience.

Wait for the Lord; be strong and take heart
and wait for the Lord.

All those seedlings I planted out in spring are growing well. The petunias and begonias are bushing out, the busy lizzies are flowering already and the geraniums are promising some great colour. Mind you, the greenfly are calling up all their friends and doing the insect equivalent of licking their lips, but that's another story.

It's interesting asking a gardener what makes a good garden. Some enthusiasts say it's the soil – rich, well-drained humus. Others say good plant stock, F1 hybrids and all the rest of it. Or regular feeding and watering, when hose-pipe bans allow. But I don't think I agree with any of them. The most important thing for a good garden is time.

Gardens aren't instant things, in spite of the impression Alan Titchmarsh and Charlie Dimmock give on television in the two-day make-overs they give to someone's patch. Gardens need time. Even Alan and Charlie return a year later to see how the gardens they have created are developing. Moving home, a friend once told me he was going to get the garden right before he did anything inside the house, because the garden would take more time. You can lay a carpet in a day, but a shrubbery needs several years. Whether his wife agreed I can't say, although they're still together.

Waiting. Saint Paul, writing to the Christians in Rome, tells them that all creation 'waits to be brought into the glorious freedom of the children of God'. But that takes time, too. A time we can use wisely, lovingly, or not at all.

Lord of creation, my time is in your hands.
Help me to grow to fullness and to freedom.

But hope that is seen is no hope at all. Who hopes for what he already has? But if we hope for what we do not yet have, we wait for it patiently.

I love good coffee and recently the family gave me a coffee-maker. It's a great machine. It sits on the work surface in the kitchen, all dark green enamel and stainless steel, with an air of impeccable good taste. And when you load it with ground coffee and switch it on, it gives a dramatic performance that is better than the telly. It gurgles, hisses and steams like a miniature volcano until that rich, dark coffee trickles alluringly into the jug below. And yes, it will produce decaffeinated, if that's what you want.

If you're in a hurry, a teaspoon of instant in a cup will be quicker, but it's nowhere near as good. The real coffee is well worth the extra time and effort it takes.

My grandchildren are at the stage where they're learning that sometimes you have to wait for things. You don't get everything you'd like immediately. I remember my mother, who never bought anything on hire-purchase, telling me in the very distant past, "If a thing's worth having, it's worth waiting for." That used to irritate me intensely, particularly between Christmas and birthdays, but it's true.

We live in an instant society, whether it's coffee or credit cards. We want everything now and some folk even think of faith that way. Yet Christian maturity is something we have to grow into. It takes time and effort and patience. But it's worth the wait. Instant holiness isn't an option.

Lord, I'm looking at my watch again,
but when my patience wears a little thin,
yours doesn't. Thank you.

*... now we are children of God, and what we will be
has not yet been made known.*

The longest running play in London's West End is *The Mousetrap*. It's a thriller by Agatha Christie and has been running for over 50 years. The cheese must be getting a bit stale, and I don't know how many generations of mice have come and gone, but the play still attracts the tourists.

I don't know who dunnit – the murder that is – but I'll lay odds it wasn't the butler. That would be too easy. Whoever it was, the audience is always asked to keep the secret when they leave. Knowing how the play ends would spoil it for those who come later.

And it could spoil everyday life too. There are times when we'd like desperately to know what's going to happen tomorrow, or next year, but there's no way we can predict it with any certainty. And if we knew, we might not like it, perhaps wouldn't be able to cope with it.

I suppose this comes from wanting to feel safe, to know where we are and where we're going. Hans Christian Andersen, the writer of those wonderful fairy stories, was born in a slum and felt insecure all his life. When he travelled, and he travelled all over the world, he always carried a rope with him – so that he could escape through a window if he was caught in a fire.

But not knowing, not being sure, is part of life. And as we start each new year, as we faced all the hype of the new Millennium, we should take life as an adventure, a pilgrimage. It's scary at times, but God is with us on life's journey (and he invented the Millennium anyway).

**When my way looks dark and indistinct, Lord, help me
to recognise that security lies not in knowing, but in you.**

Overleaf:
Paphos, Cyprus, *Watercolour*

> "Do not judge, and you will not be judged.
> Do not condemn and you will not be condemned.
> Forgive, and you will be forgiven."

I was listening to a programme on the radio the other day. An American woman was talking about her experiences as a tracker. She searched for people who got lost in the desert in parts of the USA. A little girl had wandered off from her parents as they picnicked beside their 4x4 vehicle. When they couldn't find her they called in the police, who in turn called in the tracker. The search went on all day. No trace. Her parents were desolate.

Eventually, as time was running out, the tracker heard the child's voice. She found her, alive and well. The little girl ran to the tracker, arms wide open. "I'm Mandy," she cried. "My parents got lost." That was her way of understanding what had happened.

I suppose we all do it at times. Blame the other person, I mean. Project our problems onto others rather than accepting responsibility. "It's his fault." "I never said anything." "It wasn't me, guv." Maybe a bit more honesty in the way we look at ourselves and at other people, accepting that just occasionally we might be to blame, would strengthen our relationships. And if we could include God in those relationships, maybe we wouldn't feel so lost.

Lord, teach me to look
on others with love,
as you look on me,
and to be slow
to judge them
as you are slow
to judge me.

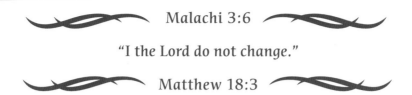

Malachi 3:6

"I the Lord do not change."

Matthew 18:3

"I tell you the truth, unless you change and become like little children, you will never enter the kingdom of heaven."

I was standing in a bus queue one day last summer. That in itself made me feel virtuous. I don't stand in bus queues very often. I'm usually taking up space on the road in my car.

It was hot, the sky blue and cloudless, the sun like bright honey. Everyone was in colourful summer frocks. Well, not everyone, only the women. It was surprising how many men were still wearing suits.

In front of me, two women were talking, complaining about the heat. "I don't like this hot weather," said one, "it ought to come gradually, so that we can get used to it." I wasn't sure how that could be arranged, but it is clear that rapid change unsettles folk. Yet that's the world we live in. And I suspect that change has always seemed too fast for those experiencing it. "I can't do with these newfangled bronze knives," said the Stone-Age man, chipping away at his flints. But things do change daily; change is the one thing we can be sure of.

Even our faith changes. Or should do. What I understand and believe now as a Christian is very different from what I believed 30 years ago. That's not because God has changed but because my experience of him has deepened and therefore my understanding has changed. And I hope that all the changes are for the good although that's not for me to judge.

The one thing that doesn't change is God's love. In the midst of change, that is one assurance which can help us cope with the rest.

Changeless Lord, you are my security. Help me to accept the changes that this day will bring and use them gladly.

> "Therefore I tell you, do not worry about your life,
> what you will eat or drink; or about your body,
> what you will wear. Isn't life more important than food,
> and the body more important than clothes?"

At a conference in Denmark I talked to a friend who had worked in a remote area of south-east Asia. He told me about someone who had taken a village worker into the city for the first time. They walked into a tall office block and needed to go to the sixth floor. There was the lift. Without thinking the man pressed the button, the lift came down and the door slid open. The villager stepped back in surprise. "What sort of room is this?" he asked, looking at the little metal box in front of him.

As my friend's colleague tried to explain, another man walked past, got into the lift and pressed the button. The door closed and the lift went up. They watched the indicator showing which floor the lift had reached: one, two, three, four. "See, it's all right," he said. "It's gone up and in a moment it'll come down again."

The lift came down. The door opened and out stepped a woman. The villager stared. "There's no way I'm going in there," he said, "if that's what happens." And he headed for the stairs.

No, I'm not sure if it ever really took place but it illustrates a point. What we don't know can be frightening. What we don't understand can be threatening. We worry and it doesn't help much when folk tell you not to. "Who says worry doesn't work?" said a man. "The things I worry about never seem to happen!"

You don't know what you're going to encounter today but the chances are that you'll be able to cope with it. But if you can't, try sharing it with someone else. And if you're really stuck, try God – he's around all the time.

> Today is unknown territory.
> Whatever it may bring, Lord of the way, stay near.

**Carry each other's burdens,
and in this way you will fulfil the law of Christ.**

Some evenings my phone rings too much. You know the feeling? You've had a busy day, eaten your meal, locked the door and settled down to watch the telly. The most energetic thing you plan to do is work the remote control. Then the phone rings – double-glazing, free conservatories, whatever.

But having a phone is more of a blessing than a curse, so I'll put up with the annoyance.

I've just been to a conference in Denmark and while I was there I wanted to phone home. Hotel phones are always expensive, so the cheapest way is to buy a phone card. They work just like the English ones. Lift the phone, put the card in the slot, dial the number and the display tells you how much time you've bought. When you've used it up, the line cuts off.

After a long session at the conference I suggested, as a joke, that the speaker should buy time on a card to limit his speech. I say his – it's usually men who go on too long at conferences.

Then I thought a bit further. If we all had to buy the time to talk ... maybe we'd talk less. Except the politicians, but we can't control them anyway. And if we talked less maybe we'd listen more. Listen to what other people want to say.

When people are worried or upset what they often need most is someone who'll give them time, by just sitting and listening. The Bible encourages us to carry each other's burdens and share the load. We can't always fix the problem, but a sympathetic ear can help.

But maybe I should practise what I preach and stop right now.

**Lord of the silence, my life is full of words.
Carve out a space for quiet in my busyness.**

And this is his command: to believe in the name of his son,
Jesus Christ, and to love one another as he commanded us.

Standard instructions you hear as the plane gets ready for take-off: "Please fasten your seat-belt and put your seat back in the upright position." Rules and regulations. 'Only eight people in the lift.' 'Speed limit 30 miles per hour.' They all make life safer when we follow them, although most of us forget the one about the speed limit. But life can't really be contained by rules. There's more to it than that.

Every day we face situations with no convenient rule to tell us exactly what to do. We have to use our common sense and make our own decisions. We're on our own. Well, not quite. There are some basics for all of us, whatever our faith. To some the Ten Commandments are old hat, but if we followed them society would be a lot better.

Then there's a rule from Confucius, "Don't do to others what you don't want them to do to you." That's OK, but Jesus put it positively. He said, "Do unto others as you want them to do unto you." It's one thing to say that you've never done anyone any harm, even if it's true. It's quite another thing to actually do some good.

The first rule is one of respect. Acknowledging a person's space, not treading on his or her toes. The other is a rule of love. Not hurting people is great as far as it goes, but love has to be proactive, if you'll pardon the jargon. It means getting out there and doing some good without waiting to be pushed.

Jesus said he had come into the world to offer us a better life. He came. He didn't hang about waiting to be asked. And neither should we, if the love that is at the heart of the universe is going to be part of our lives.

Lord of my life, teach me your rule of love and help me to
understand that it offers freedom, not constraint.

"You have heard that it was said, 'Love your neighbour and hate your enemy.' But I tell you: love your enemies and pray for those who persecute you."

The other evening I was vegetating in front of the telly. There seemed to be some noise in the background. The remote control was on a chair on the other side of the room. I thought remote controls meant you could control the telly without getting up. Now you have to get up to find the remote.

Anyway, as I got up and fetched the device, I realised the noise was coming from outside in the garden. Over the hedge and a few gardens away there was a whole disco package – lights and music. Loud music. Then a voice singing 'happy birthday' to someone through an amplifier. I was still clutching the remote control but it wasn't going to help with this. And no sign of rain – that would have been a blessing.

"Oh well," I thought, "it's only 11 o'clock. They'll stop soon." But they didn't. Bedtime came, but no sleep. There were complaints, of course, and eventually the noise did stop.

The sad thing is that we only seem to notice our neighbours when they're a nuisance. The poet T.S. Eliot wrote in his play *The Rock*:
> And no man knows or cares who is his neighbour
> Unless his neighbour makes too much disturbance.

We've little time for neighbours otherwise. We scurry around, busy with our own affairs. A recent survey suggested that about half the people in some areas don't even know their next-door neighbour's name. Jesus said neighbours were people who helped each other. Maybe if we made a bit more time for our neighbours, built up a better relationship with them, we might not have to endure noisy parties.

And if there were noisy parties, maybe we'd be invited.

Lord of the dance, thank you for neighbours,
joy and celebration.

Overleaf:
Far Horizon, *Pastel*

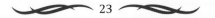

... but set an example for the believers in speech, in life, in love, in faith and in purity.

The box said 'Extra-thick baby wipes'. "Strange," I thought, "I've never seen any extra-thick babies. Chubby ones, yes, and not so chubby, but extra-thick babies? I'm surprised parents don't complain."

Then there's 'Baby Changing Facilities'. I remember having thoughts like that when our kids were six months old and crying at three in the morning, but on the whole I guess parents are satisfied with the babies they've got and wouldn't want to change them.

And on the radio the other day a presenter described a man who " ... was on crutches following an operation." I wondered where he was following the operation to? And wouldn't he have followed it better without the crutches?

It's so easy to say the wrong thing, put a double meaning where we hadn't intended to. Sometimes it's funny, but not always. It's easy to misunderstand what people say and to hear in their words meanings they never intended. And however hard we try people can misinterpret our words. And once the words are out we can't call them back.

The tongue is a bit of a problem isn't it? It's only a small part of the body but no one has been able to tame it. It's not really the tongue – it's the mind. So let's think before we speak, and when we speak, say it with love. And when we hear someone say something we don't like, give the other person a chance to explain before we sound off.

The Chinese have a saying – don't they always? 'If you want to appear wise, don't open your mouth.' Maybe that goes for me, too.

Listening Lord, may I speak less and listen more today. And in the listening may I hear the words that aren't said.

**Do nothing out of selfish ambition or vain conceit,
but in humility consider others better than yourselves.**

You should see my studio. Well no, you shouldn't really. It's untidy and that's being polite. I call it creative chaos and I know where everything is. I can find the brush and paint I need, I know exactly where my watercolour papers are stacked, and I've got just enough space around my computer to work. But that's not how it looks to anyone else and it may disturb someone with a really tidy mind. Now, though, I've got a reason for the untidiness. An excuse anyway.

I'm told that pine trees are dying in the grounds of Kensington Palace because of misplaced tidiness. Gardeners have swept up all the fallen cones and pine needles. It's all very neat but the trees are dying because the roots have lost their natural protection. Those deep layers of soft springy leaves that build up over the years in pine woods help to prevent the soil from drying out. Without them the trees suffer.

It was all done from the best of motives but it hasn't worked out very well. We need to think about consequences before we interfere with nature. Even our best intentions can go wrong. We need to think before we act.

That applies to our personal relationships, too. Good intentions don't help much if we're tactless and tread on someone's toes. 'Speaking the truth in love' (Ephesians 4:15) is a great ideal, but sometimes it's an excuse for getting rid of our anger. Not such a good idea. Engage the mind before putting the mouth in gear.

*Lord, help me to think
before I speak and then
to speak in love.*

There is neither Jew nor Greek, slave nor free,
male nor female, for you are all one in Christ Jesus.

Some time ago I went to Japan to investigate a project The Leprosy Mission was involved in. I was taken out to lunch by the Japanese man in charge. His English was a bit limited and conversation wasn't easy but at least he tried – I knew no Japanese at all.

The restaurant was set in beautiful gardens. We sat outside at a small, square table in the shade of cherry trees. The table had a small charcoal fire in the middle, glowing red. A Japanese waitress appeared in a kimono. She brought food: thin slices of fish, meat and vegetables with little bowls of sauce. Then she cooked the food on the fire and served us.

It was good. "Is this a traditional form of Japanese cooking?" I asked. My host paused, and looked at me in surprise. "Oh no," he said, "this is barbecue."

This was barbecue? I kept a straight face, although inside I was smiling. But only for a second. It's easy to make fun of things or people we don't understand, but what they had done was to take the barbecue and adapt it to their own culture. They weren't burning sausages or under cooking hamburgers like we do, but it was a barbecue – we were sitting out of doors, cooking food over a fire. It was just fine-tuned, a little different. And as a woman was doing the cooking, nothing got burnt.

It's easy to laugh when people do things differently. To think that mine's the right way of doing things, or even the only way. And from laughing at people, it is only a short step to dislike and persecution. Thank God for diversity. For different people, different cultures and the richness and variety they bring to life.

Lord of all nations, open my mind to the richness of your world
and to accept its wonderful diversity.

"Ask and it will be given to you; seek and you will find; knock and the door will be opened to you."

DIY – Do It Yourself. A friend once said that when he retired he'd make a fortune running a combined DIY and First Aid course. He reckoned that most people taking up carpentry or laying floor tiles end up cut or bruised. It's true – I have the scars to prove it.

I was hanging a door the other day and it was obeying Askew's DIY Law No. 2 which states that 'Every job takes twice as long as you think it will.' Incidentally, Askew's DIY Law No. 1 says, 'Every job is twice as complicated as you think it will be.' I've also discovered Law No. 3 which states that when you're holding up a loose door with one hand the screwdriver is just out of reach. The answer to all these laws is to pay someone else to do the job.

But I began to think about doors and what they're for. Are they to keep people out or to let people through? I suppose a bit of both really, but I think the letting through is the most important. If we simply wanted to keep people out, there would be no need for a door at all. Just block the hole up.

A door lets people in to share our space and allows us to get out into a wider world. Do you let people into your life or do you keep the door firmly shut? Jesus talked about being a door, a door to new life. An opening to richer experience. And thinking about that someone said, "When you open the door of your life to God, you find he's already opened the door of his life to you."

Lord, may I find the courage to open the door of my life to you and to throw away the key.

"Here I am! I stand at the door and knock. If anyone hears my voice and opens the door, I will come in and eat with him, and he with me."

Do you remember Frank Sinatra's classic song *My Way*? "Regrets, I've had a few ... " he begins but then shrugs them off as "too few to mention". It's a powerful song but I'm not sure that living life 'my way' is the best way. It can be selfish, can bring us into conflict, encroach on others' ground and create more regrets than we need.

Looking back at life, I too can identify things I did my way and now wish I'd done differently. Missed opportunities stick in my mind. They come in two forms: things I wish I hadn't done, and things I didn't do and wish I had. People I might have helped and didn't. Offers I never took up. Not the ones from Reader's Digest but the chance to learn more, to expand my horizons. Doors I never opened.

The poet T.S. Eliot wrote in his poem *Four Quartets – Burnt Norton*:
>Footfalls echo in the memory
>Down the passage which we did not take
>Towards the door we never opened
>Into the rose-garden.

Jesus said, "Behold I stand at the door and knock ... " That door doesn't always lead us into a rose garden, far from it, but opening it to him offers a richness and completeness to life which covers all our regrets and frees us to live life his way. Open the door.

Lord, if my door
seems shut, please
knock a little louder.
And, if necessary, push.

If I have the gift of prophecy and can fathom all mysteries and all knowledge, and if I have a faith that can move mountains, but have not love, I am nothing.

Have you got a junk drawer in your kitchen? We have. A place where we put everything that has no other home. Old gloves, bits of string, keys for locks we changed years ago. Broken pencils, used-up biros.

But there's a mystery about junk drawers. Why is it that whenever you need something from the drawer it's always right at the back, and to get at it you have to take everything else out? And why is it that when you've taken out what you want, leaving more space for the rest, there's never enough room for everything else to go back, however hard you squeeze it in?

Life is full of mysteries, mysteries even more important than our junk drawer. Love is one of them. However much we pack in there's always room for more. One of the most poetic pieces of scripture, which we often hear at weddings, is about love:

> Though I can fathom all mysteries and all knowledge ... but have not love, I am nothing.

Love is the greatest mystery of all and the thing that makes life worth living; the chemistry that draws two people together and keeps them together; the power that draws us towards God. We may not understand it, we may never understand it, but it can fill our lives to the very brim.

And, whatever cynics may say, it's not junk. Love is the greatest thing we can possess. And however much we have, however full the drawer may be, we can always pack in a little more.

Lord, sometimes my life is knee-deep in junk.
Help me to sort it out and to make more space for you.

Overleaf:
Buttercup Meadow, *Pastel*

"I have come that they may have life, and have it to the full."

I walked past a pub in town the other evening. No rude comments, please. It looked warm and inviting, all its lights on. Then I saw the painted notice on the wall outside. It said just three words: FOOD DRINK LIFE.

It sounded a great offer, but I wasn't quite sure what it meant. The food and drink I understand. Ploughman's lunch, for example – choice of stilton or cheddar, brown or white roll and a pint of bitter – but I'd like to know more about the life on offer.

My guess is that they're saying the pub is a lively place with a lot going on. Music, quizzes, friendly conversation. Nothing wrong with that, it's a pleasant way of spending the odd hour – but life? Life is a bit more than that isn't it? "A ham sandwich and a glass of best life, please." It doesn't quite work out that way, does it?

"Get a life," we say to the geek who spends all his time on the Internet and thinks his computer is his best friend. It's not enough. My life needs a purpose, something that gives meaning to today and offers me a future.

Almost next door to the pub is a church. It's a lively church. Like the pub, there's a lot going on and not just on Sunday. There's life on offer there, too, not to do the pub out of business, but to offer life with an extra meaning. Jesus said, "I've come to offer life in its fullness." An offer that can give a whole new dimension to living. The friendliness of the pub may be more welcoming than some churches but it's the life that Jesus offers that really enriches us.
Blow the froth off your life and get down to the real taste.

Lord of my life,
help me explore
its height and
depth and breadth
with you.

"How long will you waver between two opinions?
If the Lord is God, follow him ... "

Walking up the road to the artists shop the other day, I followed a man enjoying the warm weather. It was the first sunny day we'd had for weeks and his bare torso was a walking art gallery. Tattoos everywhere.

His back sported a collection of what looked like wizards and gnomes – probably characters from a computer game – and on his right shoulder blade there was a topless pin-up girl. I was surprised he didn't put that somewhere he could see it. Dragons writhed up his right arm, but on his left arm was Jesus, robed and haloed. I wondered how that one fitted in with the rest.

Which meant most to him? The dragons, the pin-up or the tattoo of Christ? We all have the odd dragon in our lives. The dark bits we'd rather not think about. Relationships too – hence the pin-up perhaps – although relationships aren't something we should turn our backs on.

And who can make sense of it all? Maybe that's what he was hoping for when the tattooist's needle was putting in Jesus. Let's hope he was more than skin deep.

I don't know whether the guy with the tattoos is listening now but I'll say thank you to him anyway for making me think.

My motives are always mixed, Lord. Strengthen the good in my life and cover the bad with your love.

If I say, "Surely the darkness will hide me and the light become night about me," even the darkness will not be dark to you; the night will shine like the day, for darkness is as light to you.

I have a continuing problem with the evil and violence in the world. Don't we all? And to be honest, I don't find that being a Christian always helps. Believing in a God of love in the face of all the rotten things that people do to each other isn't easy. Whether it's Kosovo, Rwanda or Sierra Leone, it doesn't make for a very happy scenario.

And when I try to make sense of it I have far more questions than answers. In fact, I don't have many answers at all and sometimes I'm tempted to bury my head in the sand, and try to ignore everything. But that doesn't work. Not for me, anyway.

Recently, BBC television put on a series of brief comments by its war correspondents. Most of them said the same thing in different words. "War is ugly," said one. "Terrible," said another, "dirty." Then Kate Adie came on and she was different. She said, "I am amazed at the amount of good human nature you find in the very worst of circumstances."

Now that's something I can hang on to. Ultimately, it's not the violence that registers but the fact that in the middle of it, goodness keeps popping up in the most unlikely places. And it pops up persistently. Random acts of kindness, they're sometimes called.

Writing his Gospel, Saint John says, 'The light shines in the darkness and the darkness has never put it out.' That's the antidote to my doubts. The way good refuses to go away. And come to think of it, I'm not so sure these acts of kindness are quite as random as they seem. There's something – someone – behind them.

Lord of light, sometimes it's such a struggle finding good in life. Open my eyes to your presence in my world today.

I lift up my eyes to the hills – where does my help come from?
My help comes from the Lord, the Maker of heaven and earth.

A friend was telling me about his early life as a coal miner. He'd been a Bevin boy – conscripted during World War II but sent to work in the mines instead of the armed forces. He said it was hard work, but there was a great spirit amongst the miners that carried you along. Most of the time, anyway.

But on early shift one day he was walking to the pit before dawn, feeling depressed. He wished he was somewhere else, doing something different. Life seemed pretty dull. Not much to write home about.

Then, he said, the sun rose over the slag heaps and there was more beauty in that moment than he could hold. A lovely phrase, that: 'Sunrise over the slag heaps.' A great book title – but he had it first. There's hope in it. A promise of better things. The light and warmth of the sun keeps us alive. And the beauty it creates keeps us feeling positive.

Sometimes we seem to be walking through slag heaps – seeing the dark side of life, the waste, the suffering. But the sun rises, even on rainy days, and offers us the possibility of beauty and goodness. Among the graffiti found on the wall of a concentration camp at the end of the war was one which read:
    I believe in the sun even when it doesn't shine.
    I believe in God even when I can't see him.

It's not always easy holding on to hope when among the slag heaps, but there's good waiting to rise above them. Keep your eyes open today. Beauty may appear when you least expect it.

God of surprises, life is never dull with you.
Help me to accept the twists and turns upon my road today.

Overleaf:
Akbar's Mausoleum, Agra, *Watercolour*

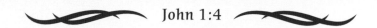

In him was life, and that life was the light of men.

Books breed in our house. Put two books together in a dark corner overnight and in the morning there are three. I'm sure of it. Every so often, we have a cull and several bagfuls finish up at the Oxfam shop. One book stirred memories. It was a book on archaeology called *Digging up the Past*. That's what I've been doing recently.

I'm just back from a nostalgia trip to India. My wife Barbara and I worked there for 15 years. Our two daughters were born in India and went to school there. So we went back and took a trip down memory lane before I was finally past it. The girls didn't put it quite like that, of course. They're much more tactful.

We began in Calcutta, revisiting places we'd known. It's a city of contrasts – forgive the cliché – wealth and squalor, high rise flats and dreadful slums. However many times you walk through the crowds, the courage and resilience of its people hits you again. So many changes, but so little fundamental change. The poverty, the struggle to survive, is still real. And it's easy to concentrate on the injustice, the exploitation, to ask why there's such inequality in the world. And I don't have an answer.

But Calcutta is the city which inspired Mother Teresa to begin her work. And that makes me turn the whole thing round and marvel at the mystery of goodness. The fact that wherever human beings create suffering goodness springs up. Wherever there is need, people are moved to put out a hand to help each other.

Hang on to the presence of goodness today and do what you can to help it to grow.

Lord of all goodness,
   let me confront wrong
   and injustice in
      your name,
   but teach me
      always to
      look for
      the good.

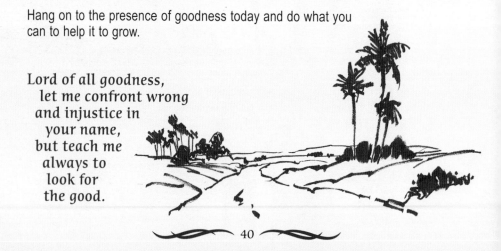

How beautiful upon the mountains are the feet of those
who bring good news, who proclaim peace.

During our trip to India, our two daughters and I went up to Darjeeling. It's
a town perched on a mountainside in the Himalayas at an altitude of more than
7,000 feet. The path in is a 50-mile mountain road, a three to four hour drive,
depending on the nerves of both driver and passengers and how many trucks
you meet on the hairpin bends. I've forgotten the Bengali for rollercoaster but
that's how it would be described in any language.

Just outside town is the boarding school our daughters attended. We took a local
taxi to it and explored. The quad, the playing fields were just as we remembered
them. Memories flooded in as we walked the school corridors and looked in the
classrooms. Jenny's desk was still where it was decades ago. And in the school
hall the footprints were still there – on the high ceiling. Years before, when the
ceiling was being re-lined with plywood, a workman must have walked over
one sheet with bare, dusty feet and no one had noticed until the board was up.
Then it was too late and thirty years later the marks are still there. Footprints
on the ceiling.

Memories. We all leave a mark on life, sometimes deliberate, often accidental.
And most of the time we don't know we're doing it. Usually it's a bit more
pedestrian than footprints on the ceiling – I'm sorry about the pun – but it is
in our power to leave a memory today in the lives of those around us. Something
positive. Something to make the world a slightly better place. Go on, do it.
You know you can.

Lord of memory, may the remembrance of your love help me
this day to live in the reality of your presence.

Surely goodness and love will follow me all the days of my life,
and I will dwell in the house of the Lord forever.

Out walking one day in Darjeeling I heard a small bus gasping and grumbling up the hilly road behind me. I flagged it down. I, too, was gasping and grumbling in the high altitude – 7,000 feet above sea level.

They're rickety, old buses in the area, held together with wire and optimism, but they still have first- and second-class seating. First class is on the front bench seat with the driver – even though four people may be squashed into the space for two. Second class is in the back with the rest of humanity and their sacks of rice, live goats and chickens.

There was no room for me up front, so I squeezed into the back with everyone else. It was crowded but very friendly. When I got out the driver asked for the fare. "But that's the first class fare," I protested, "and I've been sitting in the back."

"Yes," he said, grinning, "but anywhere you sit is first class." I gave him the extra. It was only a few pence and I thought he deserved it for diplomacy.

I know people who make everything around them first class. Positive people, whose lives radiate goodwill. And I know others who, wherever they sit, bring the quality of life down by their criticism. Jesus's message was about living life to the full. First class. Do it his way and life is all the richer. It may not explain everything that happens but it tells us that there is good at the heart of the universe, a good that we call God.

Lord of my journeying, you offer life.
Forgive me for the times I'm not quite ready to accept it.

... For your love is more delightful than wine.

Our nostalgia trip to India ended with a visit to Agra to renew our love affair with the Taj Mahal. It's a three-hour drive from Delhi, the last few miles struggling through the streets of Agra crowded with people, taxis, rickshas, cycles, creaking bullock carts and ambling camels. However many times you see it – and I've been there seven or eight times – the Taj Mahal is still wonderful. The beauty of its proportion and line, the purity of its white marble, in spite of the growing pollution, still take my breath away. And stay in my memory. Nothing like it anywhere else.

It's hard to believe that about a century ago an agent of the British government, seeing the Taj neglected, proposed that it be demolished and the marble shipped to England for auction. He felt there was money to be made. Fortunately, Lord Curzon of Keddleston saw off the idea and saved the Taj Mahal for the world.

The Taj Mahal is about memories. Shah Jahan, the emperor, was deeply in love with his wife. He should have been – they produced 14 children together. And when she died, aged 39, giving birth yet again, he was disconsolate. He built the Taj Mahal in her memory and as her tomb. What a love token. A love affair still remembered nearly 400 years later.

J.M. Barrie said, "God gave us memories that we might have roses in December." We can't all build our own Taj Mahals, we probably wouldn't get planning permission, but as you go about your life today treasure the time and the people around you. Tend your own patch of garden and encourage the roses.

Loving Lord,
strengthen my
love for you
and help me build
my life upon it.

Jesus looked at him and loved him.
"One thing you lack," he said. "Go, sell everything you have
and give to the poor, and you will have treasure in heaven.
Then come, follow me." At this the man's face fell.
He went away sad, because he had great wealth.

My family and I lived in India for 15 years. I was the manager of a large leprosy hospital – now there's a career move for you. In the early years we had no electricity. It's not easy running a hospital that way. No power for lights, X-rays or water pumps. Only oil lamps at night. So we got very excited the year electricity came.

Each Christmas we did a nativity play and that year we staged it outdoors to use the new lights. We built a brick stage, had a real fire, a real baby and real sheep borrowed from the neighbouring village. In rehearsal the sheep kept wandering. So we tied string round their necks and each shepherd held two or three sheep. The string wouldn't be noticed in the dark.

Next to the stage was a building with a flat roof. The angels, all dressed in white, climbed up a ladder in the dark and lined up on the roof. At the right moment, the floodlights were switched on and caught the angels in the glare. Very dramatic. Unfortunately, it terrified the sheep. "Baa," they went. "Fear not!" shouted the angels. "Baaa," went the sheep. "We bring good tidings!" shouted the angels. "Baaaa," chorused the sheep, and one, panicking, backed straight into the fire. As its tail began to burn, it leapt into the air, broke the string and dashed off. The other sheep followed. It was a shambles. A dozen frightened sheep dashing through a thousand people sitting on the ground in the dark.

Somehow, we finished the performance, but it took all of the next day to find the lost sheep. It wasn't the best nativity play we ever did, but it was the one everybody remembered. The thing I recall most, though, is the trouble you can get into backing away from the good news God offers us at Christmas.

Good Shepherd, when I turn my back on you, and try to run
away, go round the other side and wait for me.

"... the people living in darkness have seen a great light;
on those living in the land of the shadow of death
a light has dawned."

There were shepherds in the fields on the night Jesus was born in Bethlehem. It's only a few miles from Jerusalem and I sometimes imagine the shepherds visiting the city one day for the first time – leaving the sheep behind, of course. They fight their way through the crowded bazaars, the shops crammed with goods they could never afford to buy. Then the narrow alleys broaden and there in front of them is the Jewish Temple. Great flights of steps, marble everywhere. The courtyards crowded. Robed priests and sacrifices. And next to it, the Roman fortress, all battlements and armed guards.

On the other side of the city, not far away, is King Herod's palace. High stone walls, beautiful gates, more marble and gold. But the shepherds would only see the palace and the fortress from outside, of course. They were places of wealth and power. The only way shepherds would ever get in would be if they got into trouble and were arrested. And all they'd see then would be the dungeons.

And yet, the angels came to the shepherds in the fields as they sat around the fire shivering on a cold, dark winter's night. I'm not sure what angels are. We could argue about that all day – it leaves me in a fever pitch of apathy – but whatever they were these messengers brought the news that Jesus was born into our world.

They tell me that God is more often to be found among the poor than among the rich, and among the powerless rather than among the powerful. So Christmas is for the poor and powerless – although you wouldn't believe it when you look at the shops.

Lord of the poor, may I begin to see the world through your eyes,
and see the glory in the ordinary.

Overleaf:
Delhi Snack Bar, *Watercolour*

"For in him we live and move and have our being."

Most people who do jigsaw puzzles seem to do them the same way. They sort out all the straight bits first and try to make the framework into which all the rest fits. Then they sort out pieces with similar colours and group them together. It's not always obvious how they fit but given time and patience they make sense. Slowly the picture builds up until it is complete.

The pieces of my life tend to be like that. I can't see a complete picture, more an apparently random collection of little bits. I can make sense of some bits. They fit together and I can see one thing connecting to the next. But often there seems little reason for what's happening and all I can do is go on with what is in front of me, hoping there is a purpose somewhere. And that one day I'll see the whole picture and understand.

When you begin the jigsaw, there's a whole heap of pieces and you start by trusting that all the pieces are there. Sometimes, though, you get near the end and find that a piece is missing. It's frustrating. The picture is incomplete and leaves you dissatisfied.

Sometimes, the missing piece is God. Without his presence it's hard to pull the picture together. Harder still to make sense of life. But with him, given time, it'll come together and we'll see the big picture. Complete.

So many bits and pieces, Lord, to life. Help me to get them all together. And when I can't, to trust in you.

"Consider how the lilies grow. They do not labour or spin.
Yet I tell you, not even Solomon in all his splendour was dressed
like one of these."

One of the joys of spring is to drive down the boulevard near my home when the rhododendrons are in bloom. They're magnificent. Great swathes of colour – magenta and crimson, pink and white. It's the best way I know of encouraging drivers to keep to the speed limit on that stretch of road. Although you still need to keep at least one eye on the traffic. The flowers have finished now but they'll be back again next year.

Rhododendrons really became popular in Britain during early Victorian times. It was all through one man, Joseph Hooker – an unfortunate name today – but Hooker was a botanist and an explorer. He spent years travelling in Asia, America, you name it. He must have spent some time at home though – he had eight children and two wives – although not at the same time, I should add.

Hooker spent several years exploring the Himalaya mountains, visiting isolated and dangerous places no European had ever seen. He brought back many new flowers, including the rhododendron. And that inspired other people to go out and search for more.

You don't need all that information to enjoy the flowers but if it hadn't been for Joe Hooker we might not have them to enjoy at all. We all build on foundations laid by other people. It's the ideas and hard work of folk long gone which gives us most of the things we enjoy today. Spare a moment this morning to thank God for Joe Hooker and rhododendrons. And then thank God the creator, who organised the whole business in the first place.

Forgive me, Lord, I take so much for granted. And thank you,
Lord, for all those whose lives my life is built upon.

The true light that gives light to every man was coming into the world.

They were two rather ordinary vases of flowers. They sat at opposite ends of the table in church. They showed no flower-arranging skill – they were just simple bunches of single mauve chrysanthemums standing there modestly and quietly.

Then the clouds outside parted and the sun shone in through a window high in the church wall. It picked out just one vase. The dull mauve flowers were transformed, suddenly blazing with colour, the edges of the petals bright with light. They looked glorious, standing out from the shadowed wall behind. The other flowers at the far end of the table were still half hidden in the gloom.

It's amazing what a little sudden sunlight can do. I sat and thanked God for light and the unexpected beauty it can bring. My eyes kept moving from one bunch of flowers to the other. "Which was I?" I wondered. The dull, almost colourless flowers in the shade or was my life etched in light? A touch of light can bring new colour, new life, even new meaning to things.

So often in the Gospels Jesus talks about truth as light. About bringing light into dark places. And Jesus himself is described as 'the true light that gives light to everyone.' Let him light up your life today.

And another thing – plants can't live without light. Can we?

Lord of all beauty, shine your light on me today that I may brighten up the lives of those I meet.

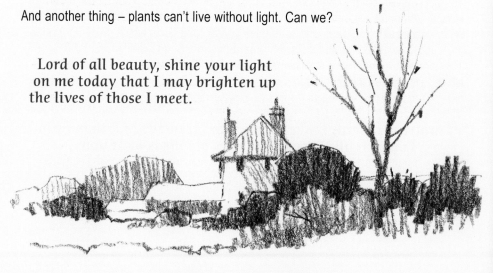

Psalm 34:1-2

I will extol the Lord at all times; his praise will always be
on my lips. My soul will boast in the Lord;
let the afflicted hear and rejoice.

Fish and chips. The original British take-away – if you discount going into the forest with a bow and arrows like Robin Hood to shoot a deer. Most Friday evenings I go down to the local fish shop for two haddock and chips. It's easy and saves cooking at the end of the week.

When I was small I had an uncle who was a trawler skipper. He was a friendly man. He seemed very old and grizzled, his face the colour of old leather. Very early one morning, he took me round the fish sheds in Grimsby docks.

I was fascinated by it all. Fish everywhere. Most packed on ice in open boxes, although some really big fish were just lying around. It was a crowded and noisy place especially when the auctioneer began to sell the boxes of fish. As we walked I kept a tight grip on my uncle's hand. I had to, my wellies had a life of their own, sliding over the wet and icy floor.

I haven't been to Grimsby for years and I've hardly thought about it. Until a few days ago, when the BBC reported the loss of a Scottish trawler, the *Solway Harvester*. Seven men, some of them only teenagers, had drowned in heavy seas. A small village community devastated. Trawler fishing is a risky business, even today with all our technology. Men risking their lives for my fish and chips and I just don't think about it.

There are so many things we should value more. Our families, the people who care for us, the love that surrounds us. All the blessings God gives us. Think about the people who work to make our lives a bit easier, more convenient, and count your blessings today. It may take longer than you think.

Lord, I thank you for the sacrifice upon which my life is built.
Help me to see the hidden love in ordinary things.

"... then choose for yourselves this day whom you will serve ..."

On holiday in Northumbria we visited Lindisfarne – Holy Island. Early Christians came across country from Iona more than 1,300 years ago and built a monastery – a place of prayer and service. Later the Vikings came and destroyed it. The monastery was rebuilt and once more invaders destroyed it. Again with quiet courage and persistence, Christians rebuilt it, strong in faith.

Later still, warriors came and built a castle high on the rocks. They spared the church but plundered the monastery for its stone. They valued swords more than prayer books. But today the warriors are just a memory and the island is peaceful, except for the raucous gulls and the sound of the sea. Even the tourists seem subdued, and half the time they can't get across the causeway anyway, when the tide is high.

And there they stand today, castle and church. The castle, high on its hill, strong and formidable, looks down on the vulnerable church below. It's a parable really, a story of power and faith. Power isolates. The mighty close the gate, pull up the drawbridge and keep people out. Behind the show of force there is fear that what they have may be taken from them. Down below the church is powerless, open to attack, but also open to all and a symbol of everything that endures.

And it is more than a symbol. It enfolds and holds a peace and a goodness that is tangible. A sign of the reality of faith and its strength in the face of whatever may come. Looking at both castle and church I know which one I choose.

Strong Lord, when weakness overwhelms me, hold me fast.
And we will stand together, you and me.

"... you are a letter from Christ, the result of our ministry, written not with ink but with the Spirit of the living God."

Recently, a friend of mine made her first visit to India. She travelled well away from the usual tourist trail and visited some villages that rarely see foreigners. Children lined up for her autograph, clutching any odd piece of paper they could find.

Why do people collect autographs? In this country it's part of a craze for collecting almost anything from old bus tickets to rare porcelain or antique furniture. But why autographs? To possess an autograph – a signature – shows that you've been in the presence of someone notable. At least it does if you collect them in the traditional way by meeting the person. And with the signature you take away something of their presence with you. Even if you buy the autograph by mail order, as many do today, you still feel you have something of that person you can keep and treasure.

Another thing. When we sign a letter or a cheque our signature shows it's authentic, genuine. Writing to Christians in the church at Corinth nearly 2,000 years ago, Saint Paul told them, 'You are a letter from Christ.' Their purpose in the world was to show to the people around them the nature of Jesus by the way they lived. And to do that they had to bear his signature. To be authentic. An autograph can be forged, but then it's not the real thing, is it?

Saint Paul wrote that 2,000 years ago but it still holds true today. The sign of the cross is the signature that tells the world we are genuine.

Lord of life, sign me
with your love,
that others may read you
in me and find it good.

Quiet Beach, *Pastel*

TLM International
80 Windmill Road
Brentford
Middlesex TW8 0QH
United Kingdom
Tel: 020 8569 7292
Fax: 020 8569 7808
friends@tlmint.org
www.leprosymission.org

TLM Trading Limited
PO Box 212
Peterborough PE2 5GD
United Kingdom
Tel: 01733 239252
Fax: 01733 239258
enquiries@tlmtrading.com
www.tlmtrading.com

TLM Africa Regional Office
PO Box HG 893
Highlands
Harare
Zimbabwe
Tel: 263 4 251647
Tel/Fax: 263 4 796155
ertlmaro@icon.co.zw

TLM Australia
PO Box 293
37 Ellingworth Parade
Box Hill
Victoria 3128
Australia
Tel: 61 39890 0577
Fax: 61 39890 0550
tlmaust@leprosymission.org.au
www.leprosymission.org.au

TLM Belgium
(Leprazending)
PO Box 20
1800 Vilvoorde
Belgium
Tel: 32 22519983
Fax: 32 22519983
leprazending@online.be

TLM Canada
75 The Donway West
Suite 1410
North York
Ontario M3C 2E9
Canada
Tel: 1 416 4413618
Fax: 1 416 4410203
tlm@tlmcanada.org
www.tlmcanada.org

TLM Denmark
Skindergade 29 A1.
DK - 1159 Copenhagen
Denmark
Tel: 45 331 18642
Fax: 45 331 18645
lepra@lepra.dk
www.lepra.dk

TLM England & Wales,
Channel Islands & Isle of Man
Goldhay Way
Orton Goldhay
Peterborough PE2 5GZ
United Kingdom
Tel: 01733 370505
Fax: 01733 404880
post@tlmew.org.uk
www.leprosymission.org.uk

TLM Finland
Hakolahdentie 32 A 4
00200 Helsinki
Finland
Tel: 358 9 692 3690
Fax: 358 9 692 4323
eeva-liisa.moilanen
   @kolumbus.fi

TLM France
BP 186
63204 Riom Cedex
France
Tel: 33 473 387660
Fax: 33 473 387660

TLM Germany
Kuferstrasse 12
73728 Esslingen
Germany
Tel: 49 711 353 072
Fax: 49 711 350 8412
LEPRA-Mission@t-online.de
www.lepramission.de

TLM Hong Kong
GPO Box 380
Central Hong Kong
Hong Kong
Tel: 85 228056362
Fax: 85 228056397
snelly@netvigator.com

TLM Hungary
Alagi Ter 13
H-1151 Budapest
Hungary

TLM India Regional Office
CNI Bhavan
16 Pandit Pant Marg
Delhi 110 001
India
Tel: 91 11 371 6920
Fax: 91 11 371 0803
tlmindia@del2.vsnl.net.in

TLM Italy
Via Adda 13
05100 Terni
Italy
Tel: 39 7448 11218
Fax: 39 7448 11218
agbertolino@libero.it

TLM Netherlands
Postbus 902
7301 BD Apeldoorn
Netherlands
Tel: 31 55 3558535
Fax: 31 55 3554772
leprazending.nl@inter.nl.net

TLM New Zealand
P O Box 10-227
Auckland
New Zealand
Tel: 64 9 630 2818
Fax: 64 9 630 0784
enquiries@tlmnz.org.nz

TLM Northern Ireland
Leprosy House
44 Ulsterville Avenue
Belfast BT9 7AQ
N Ireland
Tel: 02890 381937
Fax: 01232 381842
info@tlm-ni.org
www.tlm-ni.org

TLM Norway
PO Box 2347
Solli
Arbingst. 11N
0201 Oslo
Norway
Tel: 47 2243 8110
Fax: 47 2243 8730
gaute.hetland
@bistandsnemnda.no

TLM Portugal
Casa Adelina
Sitio do Poio
8500 Portimao
Portugal
Tel: 351 82 471180
Fax: 351 82 471516
coaa@mail.telepac.pt

TLM Republic of Ireland
5 St James Terrace
Clonskeagh Road
Dublin 6
Republic of Ireland
Tel: 353 126 98804
Fax: 353 126 98804
tlmroi@compuserve.com

TLM Scotland
89 Barnton Street
Stirling FK8 1HJ
Scotland
Tel: 01786 449 266
Fax: 01786 449 766
lindatodd@compuserve.com
www.biggar-net.co.uk
   /tlmscotland

TLM South East Asia
6001 Beach Road
#08-06 Golden Mile Tower
199589 Singapore
Tel: 65 294 0137
Fax: 65 294 7663
pdsamson@tlmsea.com.sg

TLM Southern Africa
Private Bag X06
Lyndhurst 2106
Johannesburg
S. Africa
Tel: 27 11 440 6323
Fax: 27 11 440 6324
leprosy@infonet.co.za

TLM Spain
Apartado de Correos
51.332 CP
28080 Madrid
Spain
Tel: 34 91 594 5105
Fax: 34 91 594 5105
mundosolidari
@mx3.redestb.es

TLM Sweden
Box 145
S-692 23 Kumla
Sweden
Tel: 46 19 583790
Fax: 46 19 583741
lepra@algonet.se

TLM Switzerland
Chemin de Rechoz 3
CH-1027 Lonay/Vaud
Switzerland
Tel: 41 21 8015081
Fax: 41 21 8031948
mecl@bluewin.ch
www.lepramission.ch

TLM Zimbabwe
PO Box BE 200
Belvedere
Harare
Zimbabwe
Tel: 263 4 741817
tlmzim@tlmzim.icon.co.zw

ALM International
1 ALM Way
Greenville
S C 29601
USA
Tel: 1 864 271 7040
Fax: 1 864 271 7062
amlep@leprosy.org

The Leprosy Mission Response Card

Eddie Askew is a popular Christian author and artist. His books raise funds for The Leprosy Mission to help people affected by leprosy. They are available from The Leprosy Mission in your own country or from TLM Trading Limited in the UK as well as most good Christian book shops.

TLM Trading Limited, owned by The Leprosy Mission, seeks to create employment by purchasing goods from rehabilitation centres and craft workshops who employ people affected by leprosy. These goods are sold along with gifts, cards and books to raise funds for The Leprosy Mission.

Please send me information about: - (please tick)

☐ The Leprosy Mission's mail-order catalogue

☐ The Leprosy Mission's work

☐ Prayer support

☐ Sending a regular gift by automatic payment, standing order, or direct debit to support The Leprosy Mission

☐ Tax efficient ways of supporting The Leprosy Mission

☐ Service Overseas with The Leprosy Mission

Titles by Eddie Askew

	Order Code
A Silence and a Shouting	03001
Disguises of Love	03002
Many Voices One Voice	03003
No Strange Land	03004
Facing The Storm	03005
Breaking the Rules	03006
Cross Purposes	03000
Slower than Butterflies (Book)	03024
Music on the Wind	03025
Edge of Daylight (Hardback)	03026
Edge of Daylight (Paperback)	03027
Talking with Hedgehogs	03028

Titles by Hilary Faith Jones – with illustrations by Eddie Askew

Hilary Faith Jones is a new author writing poetry that gets to the heart of the Christian faith.

Awakenings	03030
Waiting For Jesus	03031

Credit card sales and enquiries:
Tel: 01733 239252   Fax: 01733 239258
E-mail address: enquiries@tlmtrading.com

Name .... Title ....

Address ....

....

Post Code .... Country ....   Source Code 279

The Leprosy Mission (TLM) is an international Christian charity caring for people affected by leprosy. TLM was founded in 1874 by Irishman Wellesley Bailey. It is motivated and inspired by Christ's ministry of compassion to people suffering from leprosy. Working in 28 countries, with around 2,300 field staff worldwide, TLM is treating more than 200,000 people affected by leprosy through its own hospitals and programmes and those it assists.

TLM aims to meet the physical, spiritual, social and mental needs of people affected by leprosy, whilst working towards the eventual eradication of the disease. It works in partnership with churches, voluntary agencies, patient organisations, governments and international organisations to combat leprosy. It is supported by the voluntary contributions of churches and support groups around the world and has an international budget of £10 million.

Leprosy is a medical condition affecting millions of people, 90% of whom live in the developing world. It causes disability and even blindness, if untreated, by attacking nerves under the skin. It is not hereditary but is caused by a bacillus. It is not a punishment for sin! Over 95% of the world's population is naturally immune and after only a few days of treatment sufferers are no longer infectious. Leprosy can be cured by Multidrug Therapy (MDT). More than 10 million people have been cured but nearly 700,000 new cases are detected each year.

TLM Trading is a company raising funds for the work of TLM through mail-order selling. The long-term aim is to offer more items made by people affected by leprosy in order to help give employment and dignity.

The
Leprosy
Mission
International

TLM Trading Limited
PO Box 212
Peterborough
PE2 5GD
United Kingdom

Please use your local Leprosy Mission address if you prefer, see page 56.

Please
affix
stamp